THE
MEETING

BY ILYAS C. RENWICK

A wholly owned subsidiary of **TBN**

DEDICATION

To my best friend and greatest gift given by God, Danika Lynn. I love you so, and those seven "goofy" kids we partner together in parenting.

Our heroines of mothers: "Mother Hope" Renwick and the gourmet chef Dorothy "Dot" McEachern, who now serves her appetizing dishes to the Master in heaven.

And to my greatest friends: My Daddy,[1] My Big Brother,[2] and My Comforter[3]—thank You all so much for allowing me to take notes while You had Your meeting.

Yours,

Ilyas

TABLE OF CONTENTS

INTRODUCTION

FATHER.   Dearest Son, the time for fulfillment of
               the plan is at hand. The plan we have
               made….

THE WORD.   Yes, dear Father! I am ready. The plan is
               set, and *The Meeting* of the ages is ready
               to begin. Are you ready, Holy One?

HOLY SPIRIT.   …and excited! Though I have been pon-
               dering…

THE WORD.   What about, dear Friend?

FATHER.   Yes. I know what you are referring to. It
               will be necessary but let us not concen-
               trate on that now. The focus at hand is the
               Creation and the *wonderful Gift* I have in
               store for them…

   The Gift. The Gift of Life. Everyone that exists on
earth has been given this Gift. But just like any gift, there
must be a recipient. One that is *willing* to receive. The
wonderful Gift that has been given to us is *the Lord Jesus
Christ*, the Most High God (Mark 5:7); the Second of the
Triune Godhead (John 1:1; 1 John 5:7). The Precious Lamb
of God, slain from the foundation of the world (Revelation
3:8). From the moment the archangel Gabriel announced

this Gift to the world to Mary; to the announcement of His Presence in the sky via a star to the wise men, we recognize that all other gifts cannot compare to our *Lord Jesus Christ!* As God, He is the One that created you, in whose image you have been made (Genesis 1:26; Colossians 1:15–17); as man, the One who surrendered all—sacrificing His deity, power, and in total submission to the will of the Father— *His relationship with God the Father*. True enough, without the shedding of His blood, there would not be the remission of sins (Hebrews 9:22). He *had* to die in order to restore our relationship with God our Father. But He had to face rejection: of man and the very One who loved Him most... His Father.

Imagine a loved one that you have. It would pain you *to death* to be separated from them. This is what the Christ did for you—He was pained to death. Why? To understand this, you would have to understand what occurred in the wee hours of eternity at *The Meeting*.

The Meeting that occurred, which steers the destiny of mankind even now. *The Meeting* that wrote the Old and New Testaments of Holy Scripture. *The Meeting* that delivered *The Gift* unto the world.

This simple meeting consisted of three friends whose goal focused on one thing, *relationship*. The relationship that God the Father desires with His Creation. The relationship that was lost through the fall of mankind. The same relationship that is now restored through Jesus Christ's victory for us at the cross.

Father God formed the Plan of Redemption, sent the Lord Jesus Christ to consummate it, and released the Holy Spirit to seal it. It is up to us to receive it.

CHAPTER ONE
BEGINNINGS

The Meeting Is About to Begin

FATHER.   The Meeting is about to come to order. Is there any old business?

HOLY SPIRIT.   Yes, there is, righteous Father. The archangel Michael has just informed Me that the anointed cherub Lucifer has been becoming disgruntled with his duties as light-bearer. He desires more power…

FATHER.   Oh? Is that so? Hmm…

HOLY SPIRIT.   You know, this is not really a mystery to Us. His power and wisdom are second only to the Godhead.

FATHER. How are his brethren responding to this?

HOLY SPIRIT. Many are moved by his ire. A third of the hosts are convinced that he is a great leader. The rest believe that this is very dangerous indeed and are taking it very seriously.

FATHER. *(Smiles.)* Good. This is the appointed moment. This matter must be dealt with the utmost gravity.

THE WORD. It hurts Me to know this. I fashioned him to give glory to God. I did this because I love him. That is why I bestowed upon him power.

FATHER. He does have a choice on what he desires to do with that power, dear Word. We fashioned him as such. He must be dealt with immediately. For the meantime, let Us get down to business!

THE WORD. Yes, dear Father.

FATHER. I am so excited about Your plan, dear Son! Discuss it with Me. How will all of this be fulfilled?

THE WORD. Man.

FATHER.   *Man!* Created in Our image, You say?

THE WORD.   Yes!

FATHER.   Glory! This is going to be great! I am filled with joy just thinking about it. One *just* like Us! The opportunities are endless. Wait, how will man be different from the angels?

THE WORD.   They will be like Us, totally! They will have Our likeness, Our ideas, Our creative abilities. They will be able to bless and…

HOLY SPIRIT.   They will also have the opportunity to be filled…

FATHER.   Filled? With what? Filled with…?

THE WORD
AND HOLY SPIRIT.   …with Us!

FATHER.   Yes!!! This is joyous indeed!!!! Dear Friends, this exceeds all bounds! Filled with the very presence of God, crowned with honor and glory. Guys, this is great! One thing I want to add…

HOLY SPIRIT.   What is that, dear Friend?

FATHER.   I love them so much; I want to add My own special gift…

THE WORD.   Dear Father?

FATHER.   Dominion.[4]

THE WORD.   Dominion, dear Father?

FATHER.   Dominion! My children should not have the ability to be filled with Our presence without having dominion…even over the angels,[5] even considering the current situation. I want them to have the best! Nothing will be too good for them.

THE WORD.   You got it, Father; It shall be done!

FATHER.   They shall be made to have dominion over the works of Your hands; I will place all things under Your feet, all sheep and oxen; all the beasts of the field. My prized creation, I'll even give you dominion over the fowl of the air, and the fish of the sea, and whatever passes through the paths of the seas.[6]

THE WORD.   Dear Father! How excellent is Your Name in all the earth!

HOLY SPIRIT.   Dominion… That's quite a responsibility. Even considering the situation at hand.

FATHER.   The situation that must be handled immediately. Holy One, call the anointed cherub in.[7]

***

THE WORD.   How art thou fallen from heaven, o Lucifer, son of the Morning! *How* art thou cut down to the ground, which didst weaken the nations! For thou hast said in thine heart, *I will* ascend into heaven, *I will* exalt my throne above the stars of God: *I will* sit also upon the mount of the congregation, in the sides of the north: *I will* ascend above the heights of the clouds; *I will* be like the Most High. Yet thou shalt be brought down to hell, to the sides of the pit. They that see thee shall narrowly look upon thee, and consider thee, saying, Is this the man that made the earth to tremble, that did shake the kingdoms; that made the world as a wilderness and destroyed the cities thereof; that opened not the house of his prisoners? All the kings of the nations, even all of them, lie in glory, every one in his own house. But thou art cast out of thy grave like an abominable branch, and as the raiment of those that are slain, thrust through with a sword, that go down to the stones of the pit; as a carcass trodden under feet.[8]

LUCIFER.   *... (Head hung in shame.)*

FATHER.   Thou wast perfect in thy ways from the day that thou wast created, till iniquity was found in thee. By the multitude of thy merchandise they have filled the midst of thee with violence, and thou hast sinned: therefore *I Will* cast thee as profane out of the mountain of God: and *I Will* destroy thee, O covering cherub, from the midst of the stones of fire. Thine heart was lifted up, because of thy beauty, thou hast corrupted thy wisdom by reason of thy brightness: *I Will* cast thee to the ground, *I Will* lay thee before kings, that they may behold thee. Thou hast defiled thy sanctuaries by the multitude of thine iniquities, by the iniquity of thy traffic; therefore will I bring forth a fire from the midst of thee, it shall devour thee, and *I Will* bring thee to ashes upon the earth in the sight of all them that behold thee. All they that know thee among the people shall be astonished at thee: thou shalt be a terror, and never shalt thou be any more.[9]

CHAPTER TWO
MAN

"What is man, that Thou art mindful of him? and the son of man, that Thou visitest him?" (Psalm 8:4)

FATHER. How are You, dear Son? I understand.

THE WORD. I'm doing well, dear Father...thank You, my Friend.

FATHER. Holy One?

HOLY SPIRIT. Very well. It had to be done.

FATHER. We must continue. Dear Friends, what we have just done will not alter the plan. Removing Lucifer and his followers will not complicate the plan. The magnitude of the events will not alter the outcome of their future. They will burn for eternity for their iniquities, and Our wrath will be poured upon them forever.[10] Is Man completed?

THE WORD.   Man has been completed, dear Father. Here…

(The Word holds out His hand; He is holding a revolving three-dimensional image of Man with his palms out; Father God, with tears in His eyes, hugs His Son.)

FATHER.   This is beautiful. Thank you, dear Son. Man, you shall walk with Me in the cool of the day. There is nothing I shall withhold from you. You *are* My pride and joy. Your spirit shall become the candle of the Lord, and We will search all inward parts of the belly.[11] [12] Man shall be a three-part being, as We. They will *be* a spirit, *have* a soul, and *live* in a body. My secrets are reserved for you, for you are My friend.[13] Holy Spirit, I want to create something special for this gift. Let Us create a dwelling place for him, with creatures similar to what We have here. I also want Man to use Our God-given wisdom to name the creatures too. I want him to have it *all*.

HOLY SPIRIT.   Dear Father, do You want to create Man first or the creatures?

FATHER.   I want Man to enjoy what We create for him. Let Us create earth first and its firmaments, its seasons, and the creatures. Man will be designed to work. He will even help Us.[14] But I want everything to be in store for him when We create him. I love him so much to have it otherwise.

THE WORD.   Very good Father. Thy will be done.

(After the cool of the day…)

FATHER.   I am truly enjoying man, Son. Thank you so much. It is truly joyous spending time with him in the cool of the day. We talk about each other's day. I get to share all of My secrets with him. And he earnestly listens. Man is such a wonderful gift!

THE WORD.   He is so excited to tend to the garden eastward in Eden! He enjoys spending time with Us.

HOLY SPIRIT. After instructing him about the tree of the knowledge of good and evil,[15] he shudders about the prospect of *death*, being separated from God. He has vowed not to go near it. Yet, there is a hint of curiosity I've observed.

FATHER.   Yes. That must be checked. We must talk

with him at once about that. All he knows is *life*; he was not created to die, but that is what will occur if he is not obedient. His curiosity will lead to other things. Visitors...

THE WORD.   Hmm...

HOLY SPIRIT.   Dear Father?

FATHER.   Yes, dear Friend?

HOLY SPIRIT.   As I observe Adam, he seems discontent.

THE WORD.   He observes the animals he has named. He notices that there is an equal to each creature. He is pleased to be with Us, but one thing he is not...

FATHER.   Yes, dear Son, I know...

HOLY SPIRIT.   All-sufficient... I propose that We make someone for him. Someone that will complete him. One that will understand as he understands.

THE WORD.   Yes! Yes! It is not good that man should be alone;[16] I will make him a help meet for him.

HOLY SPIRIT. After he works in the garden and Our walk in the cool of the day, I will cause a deep sleep to come upon him. During that time…

THE WORD. …I will extract one of his ribs. With this rib, I will make *Woman* and bring her to him.

***

FATHER. Here, My son Adam; this is My gift to you! Enjoy.

"And Adam said, This is now bone of my bones, and flesh of my flesh: she shall be called Woman, because she was taken out of Man" (Genesis 2:23).

CHAPTER THREE
THE VISITOR

FATHER.   You *want to do WHAT*?

SATAN.   …

HOLY SPIRIT.   Surely you jest!

SATAN.   …

THE WORD.   You are a conniving, vile creature! You
                are a fool!

SATAN.   …

FATHER.   Regardless of the outcome, Satan, your
                plans will be uprooted. There is *no* way
                you will be restored to your former state.
                There is *no* way you can win. Do you
                understand that? I had thought I'd let you
                know that.

HOLY SPIRIT.   *(Smiling)* We agree. You will be punished and destroyed. No matter what the outcome is.

THE WORD.   You are granted your request.

(The deceiver leaves.)

THE WORD.   Satan detected a hint of curiosity within the Woman. That did not take long.

FATHER.   No, it did not. With him, it never does. He has had a lot of practice and plenty of time in deception. For he is a murderer from the beginning and does not abide in the Truth. The Truth is not in him. He is a liar and the father of it.[17] He deceived his brethren into thinking he was worthy of glory. He has even deceived himself.

HOLY SPIRIT.   Adam is strong. He was made thus.

THE WORD.   Yes, and although the Woman is the weaker vessel, they are both strong together.[18]

FATHER.   Yes, I agree. But Adam is just as curious as his wife. That can lead to their downfall. The command was given to Adam, the head.[19]

HOLY SPIRIT.   Yes…and with that knowledge, the enemy *will* use that against them.

THE WORD.   …and all of mankind.

FATHER.   There are three ways in which the enemy will entice them: the lust of the flesh, the lust of the eyes, and the pride of life.[20] This will be his *modus operandi* in every human's life. They should not be ignorant of this.

HOLY SPIRIT.   They are not ignorant of this. They are very well aware of this if not of You, dear Father.

THE WORD.   Will they do *Your Will*, dear Father?

HOLY SPIRIT.   I wonder too, dear Word. They have everything they need. Yet, they would they desire to eat that which We told them not to touch…

FATHER.   That is the interesting factor. The choice is Adam's. The Woman's desire will overwhelm her. Adam's desire to please his wife will overtake him. It will lead to both their and mankind's downfall. Let Us watch and see what it will be.

CHAPTER FOUR
CONVERSATIONS IN THE GARDEN

"Submit yourselves therefore to God. Resist the devil, and he will flee from you" (James 4:7).

SATAN.   *(In the guise of the serpent)* Yea, has God said, You shall not eat of every tree of the garden?

WOMAN.   We may eat of the fruit of the trees of the garden: but of the fruit of the tree which is in the midst of the garden, God has said, you shall not eat of it, neither shall you touch it, lest you die.

HOLY SPIRIT.   Very good, Woman!

SERPENT.

You shall not surely die: for God does know that in the day you eat thereof, then your eyes shall be opened, and you shall be as gods, knowing good and evil.

WOMAN.

But, I don't think…Well, I guess one little bite won't hurt; it sure does *look tasty*, so round and pretty. I believe that this fruit is the *prettiest* in the garden. In fact, I would like to take a…

ADAM.

Woman, you know what we have been told.

WOMAN.

Adam…you're right *(looking at the fruit in her hands)*. But Adam, dear, think of what *we* can have as you eat this. Your wisdom will increase; *why*, you will be able to help Father God even more.

ADAM.

He does not need any more help, my love; He *is* God.

WOMAN.

But He *did* make us for a purpose, Adam. He created you first, so there must be more that you can contribute. Please, Adam, do this for yourself, for us…*for me*.

ADAM.

The opportunity to help Father God more; I would love to do that.

HOLY SPIRIT.   Obedience is the greatest help you can give to Father God, son...

ADAM.   Why is it necessary to eat of this tree? We have all of the other trees of the garden to freely eat.

WOMAN.   Adam, my husband, this is for *both* of us. Here, I will take the first bite. If it is harmful or *if* I die, then don't eat it. I love you, Adam. But if I live, think of the possibilities!

SERPENT.   *You will be as gods...*

WOMAN.   We'll *think* as God thinks; *do* as God does...*be as God is...*

HOLY SPIRIT.   *Obedience is better than any sacrifice.*[21]

ADAM.   Obedience unto God is better than any sacrif...

WOMAN.   *(Takes a bite of the fruit and then waits to see if anything occurs.) See* Adam, *nothing* has happened! It is so *pretty* and *tasty*. I even *feel* wiser! Here...

ADAM.   No harm has come to the Woman, so I guess it is not all that bad.

WOMAN. Here, my husband, take a bite. Let *us* be wise together.

ADAM. *(Takes the bite of the fruit.)*

HOLY SPIRIT. *Adam, nooo…*

(And the eyes of them both were opened, and they knew that they were naked, and they sewed fig leaves together and made themselves aprons.)[22]

***

FATHER. Let's go, My Son. I know it hurts to see them but let Us go.[23]

***

LORD GOD. *Where are you?*

ADAM. *(Now uncovered from The Glory.)* I heard Your voice in the garden, and I was afraid because I was naked, and I hid myself.

LORD GOD: *Who told you that you were naked? Have you eaten of the tree, whereof I command-ed you that you should not eat?*

ADAM. The Woman whom *you* gave to be with me, she gave me of the tree, and I did eat.

LORD GOD.　　*(In sorrow) What is this that you have done?*

WOMAN.　　The serpent tricked me, and I did eat.

LORD GOD.　　[To the serpent] *Because you have done this, you are cursed above all cattle, and above every beast of the field; upon your belly shall you go, and dust shall you eat all the days of your life.*

LORD GOD.　　[To the enemy] *And I will put enmity between you and the woman, and between your seed and her seed; It shall bruise your head, and you shall bruise His heel.*

LORD GOD.　　[To the Woman] *I will greatly multiply your sorrow and your conception; in sorrow, you shall bring forth children; and your desire shall be to your husband, and he shall rule over you.*

LORD GOD.　　[To Adam, with tears in His eyes] *Because you have listened to the voice of your wife, and have eaten of the tree, of which I commanded you, saying, you shall not eat of it: cursed is the ground for your sake; in sorrow shall you eat of it all the days of your life; thorns and thistles shall it bring forth to you, and you shall eat the herbs of the field; in the sweat of your face shall you eat bread, till you return unto the ground; for out of it were you taken: for dust you are, and dust shall you return.*

***

And Adam called his wife's name, Eve; because she was the mother of all living. Unto Adam also and to his wife did the Lord God make coats of skins and clothed them. And the Lord God said, behold, the man is become as one of Us, to know good and evil: and now, lest he put forth his hand, and take also of the tree of life, and eat, and live forever: therefore the Lord God sent him forth from the garden of Eden, to till the ground from where he was taken. So He drove out the man, and He placed at the east of the garden of Eden Cherubims, and a flaming sword which turned every way, to keep the way of the tree of life.[24]

FATHER.   Now where there was faith, there is now fear; where there was joy, there is now sorrow; where there was encouragement, there is now discouragement. Where there was life, there is now…death.

THE WORD AND
HOLY SPIRIT.   So be it.

CHAPTER FIVE
THE BLOOD

"Much more then, being now justified by His Blood,
we shall be saved from wrath through Him"
(Romans 5:9).

THE WORD.   Man…

FATHER.   I know, Son. I know.

THE WORD.   He and his wife had everything.

FATHER.   I am saddened by it too, dear Word. But their choice to disobey was exactly that, their choice.

HOLY SPIRIT.   And though the Woman was deceived, Adam was not.[25] He received the command. He knew better. And through his line, death will reign over them, even over them that will not sin after the likeness of Adam's transgression. All will be in sin.[26]

FATHER. The course of evil affected everything so swiftly. Adam was so strong, so connected in the spirit...the spiritual realm was *even* affected.

THE WORD. He gave it over...gave it all over to the enemy.[27]

HOLY SPIRIT. Everything, man, creature, land...all creation will be tainted.[28]

THE WORD. Cursed... *(Sigh.)* I wanted to hold them so close to Me when they sinned. He took on the nature of Satan.

FATHER. Our glory covered them totally, but they took off Our glory through their choice.

HOLY SPIRIT. Yes, which is why they needed to be covered with the blood of the slain animal.

THE WORD. The slain animal, innocent...just like they were...

FATHER. I am in love with mankind, my children.

But I cannot ignore sin, for I am just. There must be something that will separate Our children from those of the enemy.

HOLY SPIRIT.   Slaying, the animal, covered them. That was the only way We could approach them... Our goodness would have slain them if We did not cover them...

FATHER.   Without blemish...totally clean and innocent of anything impure.

HOLY SPIRIT.   That's it! That will be the way We can still fellowship with them. Commune with them. Through the covering blood of animals.

FATHER.   Through this, the offender must bring certain animals slain to make atonement for their offense.[29]

THE WORD.   Yes! It will *cover* their sins! Their separation from Us. I want to touch them so much.

(The Three stand pensively silent.)

HOLY SPIRIT.   ...But that won't be enough.

THE WORD.   No, that won't.

HOLY SPIRIT.   The blood of the animals will *only* cover their sin.

THE WORD.   But they will still be impure on the inside.

FATHER.   And it still separates them from Me. Gentlemen, Satan is *not* going to win this! What will make them holy once again? I require it!

THE WORD.   …Only I can do that.

FATHER.   You…yes.

THE WORD.   The law must be established and fulfilled. They must be holy, as We are holy. Man is bound to uphold the law, which We will give them. But they won't be able to follow it thoroughly.

HOLY SPIRIT.   Yes…they are weak and will be weak. Their flesh is weak.[30] If they sin in *one* point, they sin in all.[31]

THE WORD.   I will uphold the law, Father. I will keep the law. The law can only be honored through Me.[32]

FATHER.   How will You do it, dear Friend?

THE WORD.   I will have to be like Adam…take the
             place of Adam.[33]

HOLY SPIRIT.   …What?

THE WORD.   I will have to be a…*The Sacrifice*. You
             will have to spare Me and deliver Me up
             for mankind.[34]

FATHER.   *(Pondering over His Son's words.)*

THE WORD.   It will be My destiny to pour out My
             blood for mankind. This will undo what
             will be done through first Man's fall.

HOLY SPIRIT.   Pour out Your blood? That would mean
                that You will have to become…man?

FATHER.   You will have to give up all that You
           are…

THE WORD.   *(Stands silent looking toward Man on
             earth.)* An innocent lamb.[35]

HOLY SPIRIT.   …

FATHER.   Yes, Holy Spirit. I know. But We would
           need to send Him. Even at the cost…

HOLY SPIRIT.   …of separation. *Total* separation from

God. How can God be separated from God? This is going to be something…

THE WORD.   …send Me Father. I will go. No one else is able to fulfill this task but Me. The angels of God cannot fulfill this; neither can any other creature.

FATHER.   Dear Friend, You will have to relinquish all Yourself, power—who You are…who *We* are…to become man.[36]

THE WORD.   I'm willing. And they are worth it. I love them with a perfect love. I will do whatever is necessary to bring them back. I will lay down My life and take…

FATHER.   …

THE WORD.   …Your wrath upon Myself.[37]

HOLY SPIRIT.   That can only mean one thing…

THE WORD.   I would have to become a curse,[38] I would have to become…sin.[39]

FATHER.   …

THE WORD.   Father, it must be done. I love them. You and the Holy Spirit love them, too. I must be rejected of man. I must suffer for them in order to save them. I must be disowned, dishonored, beaten...I must be...

FATHER.   ...rejected by Me.

THE WORD.   *(In tears)* But Father, the seed *must* be sown. My life as a man must be a seed. Think of the harvest. They must know that there is a way out of the mess they were put in!

FATHER.   ...

THE WORD.   Abba? (*Daddy?*)

FATHER.   Yes...I must not spare You. I must deliver You up for all of man. This way, I can freely give them all things...eternal life.

THE WORD.   Do not hold it against them. You said they are in a confused state. When it is done, I ask You now to forgive them for what they do. We know the horrors I must face...in order for this to be accomplished. Please forgive them, now.[40]

FATHER.   ...My Friend, My Son. You will have to *become* sin to undo what the deceiver has done[41] *(with tears in His eyes)*. You will have to experience...death.

37

HOLY SPIRIT. Death? You will have to experience death? *How can we?* When We are life?

(Father God and the Word look at Each Other with tears in Their eyes.)

HOLY SPIRIT. You will have to become what You are not. You will be numbered with the transgressors and have to be put to a death of shame.[42]

THE WORD. *(With tears)* Oh, Holy One. There is no other way. I must become man!!

FATHER. I have eternal life, and I want to give it. But they are sinners, and without the shedding of blood, there can be no remission (forgiveness) of sins.[43] No one on the earth is worthy of bearing the weight of their sins. Animals, though innocent, cannot bear the weight. They have also been affected ...*infected*, by the sin of man. It will run its terrible course through the whole of humanity and every creature that exists.[44] Where there was peace, there will be hostility toward man and the choice he has made.

HOLY SPIRIT. Man will sin at times and even fall short, but what will have them standing out or apart during the day of judgment?

FATHER.   I must judge sin, for I am just. I want to heal them, but a price must be paid for their total healing.

THE WORD.   As man, I will have the authority to forgive sins. I will be their escape from judgment. I will be their total healing. So, I will become man, so We can become one again and redeem them from their sins.

FATHER.   You will go not that sin might be put aside at some future time, but to put it away totally.

HOLY SPIRIT.   Will it totally undo what the enemy has done?

FATHER.   Becoming a man and doing My will completely *will* totally undo what the deceiver has done. And what he will do. How do You propose to do it, dear Son *(already knowing what is going to be done)*?

THE WORD.   My life will be the ransom for theirs...I will pay the price with My blood.[45]

FATHER.   What are we going to do about their oppression and their grief?

THE WORD.   I will be wounded for their transgressions; I will be bruised for their iniquities; the chastisement of their peace shall be upon Me; and by My stripes, they shall be healed![46] Through My death…My separation from You, dear Father…by the shedding of My blood, they shall find life. For life is in My blood.[47] [48]

HOLY SPIRIT. *(Looks at the Father, who nods His head with a smile.)* Then I am coming with you! I have a plan. Your death, dear Friend, shall be a weapon with which we shall overcome *the dragon prince*!

THE WORD. Great! Through My resurrection, death will be destroyed! Life will run its course through the veins of Our children once again!

FATHER. Yes! That will work! For by Your death, dear Friend, You will finish transgressions, make an end of sin, and bring in everlasting righteousness. My children must have it. Satan will be truly overcome through the death and resurrection of the Lord Jesus. My children will overcome him by the Blood of the Lamb, the weapon to subdue their sin against the enemy. Let's get to work on Our mission.

CHAPTER SIX
THE MISSION

"The death of Christ is the crucial point of the mission, for, with it, this is why we live. Death of Christ is the death of sin and the defeat of Satan, and the life of our hope." (C. H. Spurgeon, The Blood of the Lamb, the Conquering Weapon)

FATHER. Holy One, I understand you have a plan. What's your plan?

HOLY SPIRIT. Throughout time, I will inspire man to prepare for the coming of the Lord. The blood of animals will have to suffice for now to cover man's sins. Dear Friend, You won't be able to go until the appointed time.

THE WORD. I agree. There is much that must be done.

As You inspire man, We must send those who will listen and be obedient to Our Word. Those who will speak for us. Prophets. They will tell of My coming.

FATHER. What of the enemy?

HOLY SPIRIT. Yes. He will be a distraction but easily controlled.

FATHER. He will play on the emotion of man. He will work on their weaknesses.

THE WORD. Yes. That is true.

HOLY SPIRIT. Because of Adam's sin and making the desires of his flesh first, and not Me, man will be *very* weak.

FATHER. Yes, they will.

HOLY SPIRIT. Will they listen?

THE WORD. Not all will. Some will not listen to Us. And since they can't hear Us, many won't even listen to Our messengers, the prophets.

FATHER. True. Satan's curse will infect man so that they will reject the Truth.

THE WORD.   They will desire a lie and bondage rather than freedom.[49]

FATHER.   And Our messengers will be rejected, ridiculed, and killed.[50]

HOLY SPIRIT. But through Our prophets, I will be fire upon them, so they will not be weak. It won't be by their might or their power, but by Me![51] Those who are listening will have to give heed!

FATHER.   Good! Good! What next?

THE WORD.   All words will point to Me and My coming. I will give all the prophets witness, that through Me, whosoever believes in Me shall receive remission of sins.[52]

HOLY SPIRIT. And though the enemy is crafty, We will always be one step ahead of him. He will try to intimidate Our prophets into fear. But they will not have a spirit of fear but of power, of love, and a sound mind.[53]

FATHER.   Excellent!

HOLY SPIRIT. At the appointed time, a child, from my own heart, will be born. This child, David, will be king over our chosen people, Israel. Through King David's lineage, the

Word will come. The prophecy will be fulfilled.

THE WORD. Fantastic!

FATHER. Through the victory, My children will be set free!

HOLY SPIRIT. When they are set free, at Your command in the name of Jesus, dear Father, I will make My home in them;[54] I will nurture and tend to them, *like a garden*, and teach them Myself, by My voice, by My promptings. For I shall not speak of Myself, but whatsoever You tell me, I shall tell them. They shall become sons to Me; they shall cry to You, "Abba, Father."[55] [56] [57]

FATHER. Yes. Love will be their ears. This is only possible if You are shed abroad in their hearts. You will need to seal them, Holy Spirit.[58] [59]

HOLY SPIRIT. My love for them shall transcend time; it shall penetrate the hardest of hearts; it shall remove doubt, worry, and dispel any fear the enemy has set up—from their childhood to their adulthood.[60]

FATHER. So be it… We must get busy.

CHAPTER SEVEN
PROPHETIC SAYINGS

The scepter shall not depart from Judah, nor a lawgiver from between his feet, until Shiloh come; and to Him shall the gathering of the people be.

Genesis 49:10

And your house and your kingdom shall be established for ever before you: your throne shall be established forever.

2 Samuel 7:16

But you, Bethlehem Ephratah, though you be little among the thousands of Judah, yet out of you shall He come forth to Me that is to be ruler in Israel; whose goings forth have been from of old, from everlasting.

Micah 5:2

When you spread out your hands, I will hide My eyes from You; Even though You make many prayers, I will not hear. Your hands are full of blood.

Isaiah 1:15

He was oppressed, and He was afflicted, yet He opened not His mouth: He is brought as a lamb to the slaughter, and as a sheep before her shearers is dumb, so He opens not His mouth.

Isaiah 53:7

But yet a tenth will be in it, And will return and be for consuming, as a terebinth tree or as an oak, whose stump remains when it is cut down. So The Holy Seed shall be its stump.

Isaiah 6:13

Behold, a virgin shall be with child, and shall bring forth a Son, and they shall call His Name Immanuel, which being interpreted is, God with us.

Isaiah 7:14

Surely He has borne our griefs, and carried our sorrows: yet we did esteem Him stricken, smitten of God, and afflicted. But he was wounded for our transgressions, He was bruised for our iniquities: the chastisement of our peace was upon Him; and with His stripes we are healed.

Isaiah 53:4–5

And the Redeemer shall come to Zion, and to them that turn from transgression in Jacob, says the Lord.

Isaiah 59:20

For unto us a Child is born, Unto us a Son is given; And the government will be upon His shoulder. And His Name will be Wonderful, Counselor, Mighty God, Everlasting Father, Prince of Peace. Of the increase of His government and peace there will be no end, upon the throne of David and over His kingdom, to order it and establish it with judgment and justice from that time forward, even forever. The zeal of the LORD of hosts will perform this.

Isaiah 9:6–7

CHAPTER EIGHT
THE APPOINTED TIME

HOLY SPIRIT.   All is going according to plan, dear Father.

FATHER.   Yes, it is. Are You all ready, dear Friend?

THE WORD.   Yes. Yes, I am, dear Father.

FATHER.   Holy One, please explain the rest of the plan.

HOLY SPIRIT.   Many prophets have been sent and obediently delivered the word of their coming King and Deliverer; *the Word made flesh.*

THE WORD.   Those that did it at the expense of their lives will be greatly rewarded.[61]

HOLY SPIRIT.   *(Speaking to the archangel Gabriel.)* Good news, Gabriel! Most excellent

work! You are dismissed. Dear Friends…
the time is now!

FATHER.　　　　Speak, Friend!

HOLY SPIRIT.　The young girl Mary is soon to wed Joseph, son of David. Her father has con-
ceded to the marriage!

FATHER.　　　　I've always loved that man!

HOLY SPIRIT.　She is a blessed child…that has My heart.
She seeks Us daily and enjoys spending
great deals of time with Us. Let's give
them the most wonderful wedding present…Jesus!

THE WORD.　　How so, Holy Friend?

HOLY SPIRIT.　If You are sent now as a man, it will be
difficult for man to accept Us. Man has
had plenty of time to make mistakes;
become unstable in their ways and their
traditions. Plus, with the enemy's strong-
hold over many of their minds and lives,
the only way Our plan will work is to slip
You in as a Babe!

THE WORD.　　Excellent!

FATHER. Dear Friend, the Holy Spirit will come upon Mary, and the power of the Highest shall overshadow her.[62]

HOLY SPIRIT. The seed of man is tainted. Joseph is a child of Adam; therefore, all sinned.[63] [64]

THE WORD. Exactly! Through this, the enemy's work will be undone! For by Adam's offense, death reigned; much more they which receive abundance of grace and Our gift of righteousness, they shall reign in life by Me![65]

HOLY SPIRIT. Yes! By the offense of Adam's judgment came upon all men to condemnation...

THE WORD. By the righteousness of One, the free gift will come upon man unto justification of life![66]

HOLY SPIRIT. For as by one man's disobedience, many were made sinners.

THE WORD. So by the obedience of One shall many be made righteous![67]

HOLY SPIRIT. Moreover, the law entered that the offense might abound...

THE WORD.   But where sin abounded, grace will much more abound![68]

HOLY SPIRIT.   That as sin has reigned unto death…

THE WORD.   So might grace reign through righteousness unto eternal life by…

HOLY SPIRIT.   You, dear Friend![69]

FATHER.   Glory! Gentlemen, We are set! Holy Spirit, I will send You to come upon Mary, and the power of the Highest will overshadow her. Tell the archangel Gabriel to announce it to Mary, then Joseph. There will be much opposition, but the Lord's armies will prevail. At the age of thirty, you will fill the Word made flesh, without measure. This will come as a result of the baptism of a man named John, the Word made flesh's cousin. This man will have My heart.[70]

THE WORD AND
HOLY SPIRIT.   Done!

FATHER.   My Friends, together, We will do exploits. That devil will suffer for what he did to man!

(The Three nod in agreement.)

CHAPTER NINE
THE ANNOUNCEMENT

And the angel Gabriel came in unto Mary, and said, Hail, you that are highly favored, The Lord is with you: blessed are you among women.

And when she saw him, she was troubled at his saying, and cast in her mind what manner of salutation this should be.

And the angel said to her, Fear not, Mary: for you have found favor with God.

And, behold, you shall conceive in your womb, and bring forth a son, and shall call His Name JESUS.

He shall be great, and shall be called the Son of the Highest: and the Lord God shall give to Him the throne of His father David:

And he shall reign over the house of Jacob forever; and of His kingdom there shall be no end.

Then said Mary to the angel, How shall this be, seeing I know not a man?

And the angel answered and said to her, The Holy Ghost shall come upon you, and the power of the Highest shall overshadow you: therefore also that Holy Thing which shall be born of you shall be called The Son of God.

And, behold, your cousin Elisabeth, she has also conceived a son in her old age: and this is the sixth month with her, who was called childless.

For with God nothing shall be impossible.

And Mary said, Behold the handmaid of the Lord; be it to me according to your word. And the angel departed from her.

Luke 1:28–38

***

Now the birth of Jesus Christ was on this wise: When as His mother Mary was engaged to Joseph, before they came together, she was found with child of the Holy Ghost.

Then Joseph her husband, being a just man, and not willing to make her a public -example, was minded to put her away privately.

But while he thought on these things, behold, the angel of the Lord appeared to him in a dream, saying, Joseph, you son of David, fear not to take to you Mary your wife: for that which is conceived in her is of the Holy Ghost.

And she shall bring froth a Son, and you shall call His Name JESUS: for He shall save His people from their sins.

Matthew 1:18–21

CHAPTER TEN
BIRTH OF THE DELIVERER

"For unto us a Child is born, Unto us a Son is given; And the government will be upon His shoulder."

(Isaiah 9:6)

The Savior has just been born. Joseph watches the Savior of the world sleeping snuggly in the arms of His chosen mother. Gazing lovingly into his wife's eyes, he speaks:

JOSEPH.   Mary…

MARY.   Joseph…

JOSEPH.   How are you feeling, my love?

MARY. I am doing well, my dear. This really is something…

JOSEPH. Yes…yes, it is.

MARY. The Savior of the world, in my arms.

JOSEPH. Hmm…

MARY. Ishi? (interpreted, *my husband?*) Is everything well?

JOSEPH. Everything is well, isha—*my wife*; you rest now, with *Jesus*. I'm going to step outside for a moment.

Overwhelmed in his thoughts over what his wife had just said, Joseph looked into the star-filled sky, each ringing with the announcement across the universe of the birth of the Savior, the birth of God in the flesh, the Creator of the universe. Overtaken with this task of raising this Holy Child, Joseph sang a Psalm to God.

***

Dear Father, please hear my prayer.

It's Your servant Joseph, and this one's rare.

It's about my Son, the Savior of the world,

The One, named Jesus, birthed to me, and Mary, my girl.

The joy of this moment fills our hearts with pleasure,
With energy that touched the shepherds of the desert,
We are all excited, though one thing's puzzling,
How do I teach the One Who's created me?

How do I teach the One,
Who spans the universe with His hands,
To hold a stick,
When He's playing with His friends?

How do I raise Him,
In the admonition of the law,
When He is the One,
Who has established it all?

To feed the One,
Who feeds me,
To nurture the One,
Who nurtures me?

Do I chastise Him?
Will He be out of hand?
Dear Lord, I need help.
Hear the prayer of Your friend.

You promised me, Lord,

To care of me;

But how am I qualified...

To take care of...Thee?

Slightly overwhelmed, Joseph pondered on these thoughts as he gazed in the eastern sky of early morning. He immediately sensed an overwhelming confirmation as he heard the words in his heart: *Do not fret, dear son. I will teach you how to raise Me.*

Joseph walked back into the stables, where his wife was fast asleep with the Holy Child in her arms. Jesus reached out His stubby little fingers for His earthly father. Joseph gave Him his finger. The Child giggled and cooed. Joseph was comforted.

***

HOLY SPIRIT.   I see...yes, archangel Michael. I need you to fight. Go forth with your angels and smite the enemy's forces. Father God, I need to tell the wise men.

FATHER.   Yes, Holy One, I know. Ever since wise men left King Herod's court and the chief priests and scribes explained the Holy Scriptures to him, he's been on edge.

HOLY SPIRIT.   He does not understand that his coming king is here.

FATHER.   And he will not. His eyes have been

blinded, and his mind clouded.[71] Holy One, tell the wise men to not return to Herod. They must depart to their own country. Let them know to go the other way.[72] Michael's second forces will give them safe passage.

HOLY SPIRIT. Very good Father. And Joseph?

FATHER. Send the Messenger to Joseph in a dream.[73] Now My Son is of age; behold, the enemy has filled Herod's heart with jealousy and hatred. He will send his assassins in an attempt to take him out. Inform Joseph also that he has everything he needs financially to take his family to Egypt; We made sure of this with the gifts of the wise men. We will load him daily with our benefits.[74]

HOLY SPIRIT. Immediately?

FATHER. Yes. His life depends on it. For out of Egypt, I will call My Son.[75] [76]

***

Then Herod when he saw that he was mocked of the wise men, was exceeding angry, and sent forth, and slew all the children that were in Bethlehem, and in all the coasts thereof, from two years old and under, according to the time which he had diligently inquired of the wise men.

Then was fulfilled that which was spoken by Jeremiah the prophet, saying, In Rama was there a voice heard, lamentation, and weeping, and great mourning, Rachel weeping for her children, and would not be comforted, because they are not.

Matthew 2:16–18

***

FATHER.   Send forth the Messenger again, instructing Joseph to go into the land of Israel: for they are dead which sought the young Child's life.[77]

HOLY SPIRIT.   Joseph has been speaking to Me, dear Father. He is still a little afraid of what can occur. The account of the massacre has spread to the uttermost parts of the earth.

FATHER.   Yes. Archelaus, Herod's son, does have his father's heart. Different things he has seen his father do, he'll attempt too. I will make the crooked paths straight in Galilee. Tell the angels to go forth and make a hedge of protection around them. They must have it.

HOLY SPIRIT.   Very good. Joseph and his family shall go to the parts of Galilee and dwell in the city, Nazareth. That the scriptures might be fulfilled which was spoken by the prophets, He shall be called a Nazarene.[78]

CHAPTER ELEVEN
TEMPTATION

FATHER.   The time has come, Holy One.

HOLY SPIRIT.   For the infilling.

FATHER.   Yes. My Son is going to need You for the upcoming battles.

HOLY SPIRIT.   The temptation…

FATHER.   For this situation, too.

HOLY SPIRIT.   The enemy is going to try to appeal to His humanity. Satan is going to attack Him through His flesh.

FATHER.   The same tactic he used against the first man, Adam, and his wife, Eve.

HOLY SPIRIT.   There is nothing new under the sun, dear

Friend.[79]

FATHER.   Yes. So true, dear Friend. The enemy
              knows that he cannot attack Jesus in the
              spirit. So he'll try to uproot Jesus in the
              flesh. We must instruct My Son to go on
              a fast. He's going to need You; You must
              go now. I'll let Him know that I am well
              pleased with Him.

HOLY SPIRIT. Very good, dear Father.

                        ***

*And Jesus, when HE was baptized, went immediately out
of the water: and, lo, the heavens were opened to Him,
and he (John) saw the Spirit of God descending like a
dove, and lighting upon Him:*

*And lo a voice from heaven, saying, This is my beloved
Son, in whom I am well pleased.*

Matthew 3:16–17

*Then was Jesus led up of the spirit into the wilderness to
be tempted of the devil.*

*And when He had fasted forty days and forty nights, He
was afterward hungry.*

*And when the tempter came to Him, he said, If You be the
Son of God, command that these stones be made bread.*

*But He answered and said, It is written, man shall not live
by bread alone, but by every Word that proceeds out of the*

mouth of God.[80]

Then the devil takes Him up into the holy city, and sets Him on a pinnacle of the temple, and says to Him, If You be the Son of God, cast Yourself down: for it is written, He shall give His angels charge concerning You: and in their hands they shall bear You up, lest at any time You dash Your foot against a stone.[81]

Jesus said to him, It is written again, you shall not tempt The Lord your God.[82]

Again, the devil takes Him up into an exceeding high mountain, and shows Him all the kingdoms of the world, and the glory of them; and says to Him, All these things will I give You [and the glory of them: for that is delivered to me; and to whomsoever I will give it],[83] *if You will fall down and worship me.*

Then says Jesus to him, Get you from here, satan: for it is written, you shall worship The Lord your God, and Him only shall you serve![84]

Then the devil leaves Him, and behold, angels came and ministered to Him.

Matthew 4:1–11

***

And there was delivered unto him the book of the prophet Isaiah. And when he had opened the book, he found the place where it was written,

the spirit of the Lord is upon me, because he hath anointed me to preach the gospel to the poor; he hath sent me to heal the brokenhearted, to preach deliverance to the captives, and recovering of sight to the blind, to set at liberty them that are bruised,

To preach the acceptable year of the Lord.

and he closed the book, and he gave it again to the minister, and sat down. And the eyes of all them that were in the synagogue were fastened on him.

and he began to say unto them, this day is this scripture fulfilled in your ears.

Luke 4:17–21

***

FATHER.   Well done, Son, well done indeed. The best is yet to come.

CHAPTER TWELVE
MEETING IN PRAYER

And when it was evening, His disciples came to Him, saying, This is a desert place, and the time is now late; send the multitude away, that they may go into the villages, and buy themselves food.

But Jesus said unto them, They Need Not Depart; Give Them To Eat.

And they said to Him, We have here but five loaves, and two fishes.

He said, Bring Them Here To Me.

And He commanded the multitude to sit down on the grass, and took the five loaves, and the two fishes, and looking up to heaven, He blessed, and broke, and gave the loaves to His disciples, and the disciples gave them to the multitude.

And they did all eat and were filled; and they took up of the fragments that remained twelve baskets full.

And they that had eaten were about five thousand men, besides women and children.

Matthew 14:15–21

And straightway Jesus constrained His disciples to get into a boat, and to go before Him unto the other side, while He sent the multitudes away. And when He sent the multitudes away, He went up into a mountain privately, to pray:

JESUS.   Dear Father, it has been quite a day!

FATHER.   Son! How goes it?

JESUS.   Everything is great…just weary. The Spirit is willing, but the flesh is definitely weak. I'm so glad the Holy Spirit is here…

FATHER.   I miss You too, Son. Our children are all worth it, though.

JESUS.   Yes, Dad, they most certainly are. What is next, dear Father?

FATHER.   Just rest now, Son. Rest in my presence. Let My Holy Spirit restore You.

HOLY SPIRIT.   Most wonderful things are yet to come.

JESUS.   Yes, dear Father, and tragic.

FATHER.   Speak, Son.

JESUS.   Those who are supposed to know the

Scriptures that tell of My coming in
the law of Moses, the prophets, and the
Psalms, are the same ones that are reject-
ing Me.

HOLY SPIRIT.   And those who reject the law and order
are the ones who accept you, Lord Jesus.

FATHER.   That is understandable, dear Friends. For
it is not that which goes into the mouth
that defiles a man, but that which comes
out of the mouth; this defiles a man. The
truth needs to be told. Every plant which I
have not planted shall be rooted up.[85]

JESUS.   The Pharisees are the blind leading the
blind.

HOLY SPIRIT.   And if the blind lead the blind, both shall
fall into the ditch.[86]

FATHER.   We know those that are Ours, dear
Friends. Continue to spread the Word.
The time comes quickly when they will
not endure sound doctrine.

JESUS.   Of the twelve…

FATHER.   Peter?

JESUS.   That Peter is impressive!

HOLY SPIRIT.   Absolutely! I love his passion!

FATHER.   He tries so hard to please Us. I love him dearly.

HOLY SPIRIT.   He will lead the disciples soon.

FATHER.   Yes…

JESUS.   The time is coming, dear Father. My time here is almost over. Have I pleased you?

FATHER.   Yes, I know, dear Son. And yes, You have pleased Me! Go to Our disciples, now. Stay encouraged, for I am with You, Son.

JESUS.   That is the confidence that I have in You.

FATHER.   I love You, Son.

JESUS.   I love You, Dad.

CHAPTER THIRTEEN:
BREATH-TAKING EXPERIENCE

FATHER.   The blind see...

HOLY SPIRIT.   The deaf hear...

JESUS.   The lame are made to walk again.

FATHER.   The Word is received. The Truth is be-
                     ing told. There is a way back to me. It is
                     through My Son, the Lord, and Savior
                     Jesus Christ!

HOLY SPIRIT.   The children know to come to You, dear
                     Father.

JESUS.   Yes! The day is coming when they shall
                     ask *You* their questions, Father...in My
                     name! They'll no longer have to go

through an intermediary, for You Yourself love them![87]

FATHER. And when they ask, I will give it to them, that their joy may be full.[88]

HOLY SPIRIT. The relationship is being restored.

FATHER. Dear Son, I am so proud of You. Man knows that I love them with a perfect love because they love You and believe that You came out from Me.

HOLY SPIRIT. Jesus, You have done it! The greatest bridge in history has been restored.

JESUS. …

HOLY SPIRIT. The wonderful Gift has been given…

JESUS. Not quite. The Greatest Gift has not been given yet.

HOLY SPIRIT. I know, dear Friend. I know. It will please the Father.

JESUS. I have a request, dear Father.

FATHER. Speak Son, Your Father is listening.

JESUS.

Father, the hour is come; to glorify Your Son, that Your Son also may glorify You.

As You have given Him power over all flesh, that He should give eternal life to as many as You have given Him.

And this is life eternal, that they might know You the only true God, and Jesus Christ, whom You have sent.

I have glorified You on the earth: I have finished the work which You gave Me to do.

And now, O Father, glorify You Me with Your own self with the glory which I had with You before the world was.

I have manifested Your Name to the men which You gave Me out of the world: Yours they were, and You gave them Me; and they have kept Your Word.

Now they have known all things whatsoever You have given Me are of You.

For I have given to them the words which You gave Me; and they have received them, and have known surely that I came out from You, and they have believed that

You did send Me.

I pray for them: I pray not for the world,
but for them which You have given Me;
for they are Yours.

And all Mine are Yours, and Yours are
mine, and I am glorified in them.

And now I am no more in the world, but
these are in the world, and I come to You.
Holy Father, keep through Your Own
Name those whom You have given Me,
that they may be one, as We Are.

While I was with them in the world, I
kept them in Your name: those that You
gave Me I have kept, and none of them
is lost, but the son of perdition; that the
scripture might be fulfilled.[89]

And now come I to You; and these things
I speak in the world, that they might have
My joy fulfilled in themselves.

I have given them Your Word, and the
world has hated them because they are
not of the world, even as I am not of the
world.

I pray not that You should take them out

of the world, but that You should keep them from the evil.

They are not of the world, even as I am not of the world.

Sanctify them through Your Truth: Your Word is Truth.

As You have sent Me into the world, even so, have I also sent them into the world.

And for their sakes, I sanctify Myself, that they also might be sanctified through the truth.

Neither pray I for these alone, but for them also which shall believe on Me through their word;

That they all may be one; as You, Father, are in Me, and I in You, that they also may be one in Us: that the world may believe that You have sent Me.

And the glory which You gave Me I have given them; that they may be one, even as we are one:

I in them, and You in Me, that they may

be made perfect in one; and that the world may know that You have sent Me, and have loved them, as You have loved Me.

Father, I will that they also, whom You have given Me, be with Me where I am; that they may behold My glory, which You have given Me: for You loved Me before the foundation of the world.

O Righteous Father, the world has not known You: but I have known You, and these have known that You have sent Me.

And I have declared to them Your name and will declare it: that The Love where-with You have loved Me may be in them, and I in them.[90]

FATHER: Yes, dear Son. You shall have it, both now and forever.

CHAPTER FOURTEEN
THE DARKEST DAY IN HISTORY

Then comes Jesus with them to a place called Gethsemane, and says to the disciples, Sit you here, while I go and pray yonder.

And He took with Him Peter and the two sons of Zebedee and began to be sorrowful and very distressed.

Then says He to them, My soul is exceeding sorrowful, even to death: tarry you here, and watch with Me.

And He went a little farther, and fell on His face, and prayed, saying, O My Father, if it be possible, let this cup pass from Me: nevertheless not as I will, but as You will.

And He comes to the disciples, and finds them asleep, and says to Peter, what, could you not watch with Me one hour? Watch and pray, that you enter not into temptation: the spirit indeed is willing, but the flesh is weak.

He went away again the second time and prayed, saying, O My Father, if this cup may not pass away from Me, except I drink it, Your will be done.

And He came and found them asleep again: for their eyes were heavy.

And He left them, and went away again, and prayed the third time, saying the same words.[91]

Matthew 26:36–44

***

HOLY SPIRIT. On His own.

FATHER. Michael, you and your angels are not to interfere.

MICHAEL. I'm sorry, Father. I don't understand. Our Lord Jesus is to become *what*?

FATHER. Sin.

MICHAEL. He is to become "sin"?

HOLY SPIRIT. Yes. And He is to go to hell.

MICHAEL. That would mean that Satan would get the upper hand! I cannot allow that!

GABRIEL. Michael, this is something I don't understand as well; but Jesus is God, and that will not change.

FATHER. I called this meeting with you two because there are going to be some things you are going to see that are going to shock you.

Jesus will lay down His life for man.

HOLY SPIRIT. Heavenly Hosts, understand that this is the only way.

FATHER. The enemy believes that he will have the upper hand, but he does not.

MICHAEL. Dear Father, why? We are ready to fight on our Lord's behalf. You created us to fight—and fight we must!

HOLY SPIRIT. Yes. I understand that Michael, but you are first created to obey.

GABRIEL. Michael, dear Brother, I understand your pain. We must remain silent.

MICHAEL. *(In tears)* But Brother Gabriel…He's my Lord…

FATHER. Your Lord Jesus, my Son, has the power to take His life back.

HOLY SPIRIT. Through this victory, dominion will be given back to man. The Lord Jesus Christ laying down His life for mankind is the

Greatest Gift ever given. I will have it no other way.

MICHAEL.   Neither will Jesus…*(sniffles)*…can…can I see Him?

FATHER.   Yes. Yes, Michael. Go to Him.

"And there appeared an angel to Him from heaven, strengthening Him[92]" (Luke 22:43).

***

"Woman—I do not know the man; Man —I am not he {Peter}; Man—I know not what thou sayest—And immediately, the cock crew."[93]

Crucify Him! Crucify Him![94]

"Prophesy, who is it that struck You?"[95]

"Are You the Christ?"[96]

If I tell you, you will not believe: and if I also ask you, you will not answer Me, nor let Me go. Hereafter shall the Son of Man sit on the right hand of the power of God.[97]

"I find no fault in this Man."[98]

"Away with this Man, and release Barabbas, *the murderer*!"[99]

Father forgive them, for they know not what they do.[100]

They spit upon Him, and took the reed, and smote Him on the head.[101]

"Why, what evil has He done?"[102]

Daughters of Jerusalem, weep not for Me, but weep for yourselves, and for your children.[103]

'This Is The King Of The Jews.'[104]

Eli, Eli, Lama Sabachthani?[105]

"If you be Christ, save Yourself and us!"[106]

"This Man has done nothing wrong."[107]

"Lord, remember me when You come into Your Kingdom."[108]

Verily I say to you, today shall you be with Me in paradise.[109]

Father, into Your hands I commend My Spirit.[110]

***

FATHER.   It is finished.[111]

HOLY SPIRIT.   Yes indeed, Father, it is.

CHAPTER FIFTEEN
RESURRECTION

The angels are cheering. The creatures of God are yelling. Full realization of the current events filled *heaven*. Father God and the Holy Spirit wait for Jesus at the gates of heaven. In hell, the fallen angels were having a celebration. Satan believed that he had won. The devils in hell brought Jesus bound before the unholy throne room of hell.

SATAN. "Son of God"… ha ha ha! What have You to say for Yourself?

JESUS. He is brought as a lamb to the slaughter…He was taken from prison and from judgment: and who shall declare His generation? For he was cut off out of the land for the living: for the transgression of my people was He stricken…Yet it pleased the Lord to bruise Him; He has put Him to grief…shall make His soul an offering for sin, He shall see His seed, He shall prolong His days, and the pleasure of the

Lord shall prosper in His hand.[112]

SATAN.   Oh, no…

In all his tenacity for doing away with this Man, Satan himself was blinded. He had forgotten the Scriptures! He then realized that all the sins of mankind, from past and present, have been sucked away and placed upon Jesus, the *ultimate* sacrificial Lamb. In horror, Satan realized that he made a grave mistake. The Holy Scriptures came back to his remembrance, Jesus smiles at the enemy, and with fire in His eyes, He slaps him and yells:

JESUS.   *Satan, you HAVE LOST!*

Jesus broke free from the bonds the enemy put Him in and shone brighter than 10,000 suns in full strength! The power of God has raised Him from the dead! Hell is at its brightest as the heavenly armies break forth, standing with their Lord and Master. They are led by Michael, the archangel and general of the Warrior Hosts.

MICHAEL.   *Now, sir?*

JESUS.   *NOW, MICHAEL.*

Michael.   *Heavenly hosts of heaven, fight for your*
            LORD and KING!

Michael and his angels unleashed an attack upon the
angels of darkness unlike there ever was! In every aspect,
they had the upper hand. In the midst of the fighting, Jesus
walked up to Satan, who cowered down in fear. He rips the
authority of death, hell, and the grave from Satan's hands.
The devils in hell are in horror when they realize what was
done. For if they had known, they would have never had
crucified *the Lord our Savior, the Lord of glory.*[113]

***

FATHER.   I am so excited! I can't wait to get My
               Son back here! I missed Him so much!

HOLY SPIRIT.   Yes! The thirty-three years did go by so
               fast.

FATHER.   True enough, dear Friend. But any mo-
               ment spent away from My Son is an eter-
               nity.

HOLY SPIRIT.   I feel the same about man…

FATHER.   Yes. Hey, listen:

***

JESUS.   But wait for the promise of the Father,
               which you have heard of Me. For John

85

truly baptized with water, but you shall be baptized with the Holy Ghost not many days from now.

DISCIPLES. Lord, will You at this time restore again the kingdom to Israel?

JESUS. It is not for you to know the times or the seasons which the Father has put in His own power. But you shall receive power, after that…

HOLY SPIRIT. I love this part!

JESUS. …The Holy Ghost is come upon you, and you shall be witnesses to Me both in Jerusalem, and in all Judea, and in Samaria and to the uttermost part of the earth.[114] Go ye therefore, and teach all nations, baptizing them in the name of the Father, and of the Son, and of the Holy Ghost; teaching them to observe all things whatsoever I have commanded you: and, lo, I am with you always, even to the end of the world.[115]

CHAPTER SIXTEEN
FAMILY REUNION

And when He had spoken these things, while they beheld, He was taken up; and a cloud received Him out of their sight. And while they looked steadfastly toward heaven as He went up, behold, two men stood by them in white apparel, which also said, You men of Galilee, why stand you gazing up into heaven? This same Jesus, which is taken up from you into Heaven, shall so come in like manner as you have seen Him go into heaven.[116]

HOLY SPIRIT.   Showtime!

FATHER.   Hey! There's My Son now!

JESUS.   Father! Holy Spirit!

The Friends run toward Each Other, hugging abundantly. Jesus knelt before the Father, presenting His submission to the Father's Will, and presented all of the shed blood of Calvary to Him to be poured over the mercy seat of heaven. Father God received it as the eternal sacrifice and acknowledged the offering. He then smiled, picked up His Son, and held Him tightly.

FATHER. Son! You've done it! I'm so proud of You! You've won the victory for man! You've won the victory for Us!

HOLY SPIRIT. You're the Greatest!

JESUS. Father! Holy Spirit! Thank You, dear Friends. It's wonderful to be back. Let Me take it all in.

FATHER. You do that, Son. Let's go back to the throne.

**

(The Three Friends are laughing and enjoying Each Other's company again.)

FATHER. *(Father God is laughing with the heartiest laughter, one that resounds the hallowed halls and streets of heaven.)* Holy One, did You see the expression on the foul prince's face?

HOLY SPIRIT. Especially when Jesus whipped him in the front of the other fallen angels! And when He took the keys from him in hell?

(Hahaha!)

FATHER. Had Satan had known what he was doing or getting involved with, he would have never desired to crucify You, Lord Jesus![117]

HOLY SPIRIT. The victory was through the Blood of the Lamb being shed!!! The Eternal Sacrifice has been offered! Our kids will do exploits![118]

JESUS. …The worst part about it was being separated from You.

FATHER. It was for Me too, Son, but I commended My love toward man, in that, while man was yet in sin, I had to send You to die for man. But now! Now, dear Son, man is now justified by Your blood, which You presented to Me. They shall be saved from My wrath through You.

HOLY SPIRIT. Man was Our enemy, but they are now reconciled to Us by Your death, Lord Jesus. Rather, saved by Your life! And they now have totally received The Atonement.[119]

JESUS. And think of the wonderful harvest that has resulted from it!

HOLY SPIRIT. Yes, My Friend! Think…the birth, the death, the burial, and the resurrection; man is worth it all.

JESUS. I'd do it again for man!

HOLY SPIRIT. Glory it is completed.

JESUS AND
FATHER. Amen.

JESUS. Holy One, there's quite a work that needs to be done.

FATHER. Yes, there is.

HOLY SPIRIT. All set? Let Me at them! I'm ready to fill them!

CHAPTER SEVENTEEN
THE CHOICE

JESUS.   It is great to be back. But I keep thinking...

FATHER.   What is it, dear Son?

JESUS.   All that was done... All that they are doing now. They are walking in Our power, Our authority, The Anointing. They are turning the world upside down.

FATHER.   Yes, Son. Isn't it great! Women received their dead raised to life again: and others are tortured, not accepting deliverance.

JESUS.   That they might obtain a better resurrection.[120]

FATHER.   And others had a trial of cruel mockings and scourgings, bonds, and imprisonment.[121]

JESUS.   Stoned, sawn asunder, tempted, slain with the sword: wandering around in sheepskins and goatskins; destitute, afflicted, tormented...[122]

FATHER.   The world is not worthy of these, Son.

JESUS.   So true, dear Father. Even now, they wander in deserts, and mountains, and dens, and caves of the earth.[123]

FATHER.   These all have obtained a good report through faith, received not The Promise.[124]

JESUS.   We have provided some better thing for them, that they in the world should not be made perfect.[125]

FATHER.   Speak, Son.

JESUS.   I want to go back for My children, dear Father. I want them to be with Us.

FATHER.   I do too, Son.

JESUS.   Can You tell Me when I am going to re-
                  turn for them?

FATHER.   No, dear Son. I cannot.

JESUS.   Dearest Father, can I know why?

FATHER.   I seek true worshipers, those that will
                  worship Me in Spirit and Truth.[126] You
                  did the work, dear Son. Our family, those
                  who have accepted Me, are sharing the
                  Word with the world. Those who hear
                  have the choice.

JESUS.   I do not want any of them to die!

FATHER.   It is not My will that any of them should
                  perish, but that all should come to repen-
                  tance.[127]

JESUS.   Father, they are My…Our most prized
                  possession! All of the treasures in heaven
                  cannot even measure to mankind, Our
                  creation! They are so precious in Our
                  sight! They are a part of Us, as We are a
                  part of them. To turn them away is to turn
                  a part of Us away…

FATHER.   *(Looking at His Son in love, with tears in
                  His eyes.)* I understand Son, for I hurt as
                  You hurt, as Our Holy Spirit grieves—*for*

93

We Are One.[128] Yet, as We have created man in Our very Own image, We have given them a *will*—to love, as I love You, as You love them, as We love one another.[129]

JESUS.   Can you tell Me when any of this will take place?

FATHER.   No Son, Our love for mankind is so strong, it would be revealed. We want them to be ready because *they want* to be ready because they love Us as we love them. They must want to serve us and be ready for Your coming…Our coming. Not because of an ultimatum of the impending judgment to come, but because of love.[130]

(Jesus just cried as He looked at the Father.)

FATHER.   At that time, I will wipe away all tears from off all faces. Including Yours, dear Son.[131] [132] Then the words I have spoken through Paul[133] will come to pass…the choice is up to them.

JESUS AND
HOLY SPIRIT.   All power, majesty, and honor, and glory derives from You, dear Father! For We are a part of You and You of Us, for We are One.

94

THE CHOICE

Your will be done! The choice is up to them…

EPILOGUE

Atonement: overcoming a very serious breach between two parties.

This is what Jesus did for us. He became the bridge between God and man. Between life and death.

The Word of God said best: "For God so loved the world, that He gave His only begotten Son, that whosoever believes in Him should not perish, but have everlasting life" (John 3:16). Father God did not send Jesus into the world to condemn the world, but that through Him, the world might be saved. There is no other name here on this earth by which we can be saved other than through the name Jesus Christ. There are many decisions, *only one true choice*. What choice will you make?

It's easy. Let me help you. The Word of God declares that "If we shall confess our sins, He is Faithful and Just to forgive us our sins, and to cleanse us from all unrighteousness" (1 John 1:9). We've all sinned and were destined for spiritual death. God made the way of escape, and it's only through Jesus.

The Word also declares that "If you confess with our mouth the Lord Jesus, and believe in your heart that God has raised Him from the dead, you shall be saved... for whosoever shall call upon the name of the Lord shall be saved" (Romans 10:9, 13). It's a personal choice, only one that *you* can make.

Make Jesus your Savior today. Know this, any

moment He has to spend away from you is an *eternity* for Him. If You haven't made Jesus Your Lord and Personal Savior, please pray this simple prayer:

Dear Father, I acknowledge that I am a sinner. I repent of my sins. I recognize that there is no other way to You but through Jesus Christ. Thank You so much for sparing my life to recognize this. Lord Jesus, I accept You in my heart. I need you, and I love you. Thank You for laying Your life down, so I won't have to die in my sins. I confess You as Lord and Savior, and I believe in my heart that God raised You from the dead. Thank You, for I am now saved. Your Word declares that Your Holy Spirit is a gift. I receive this gift now. Holy Spirit, fill me now. In Jesus' name, Amen.

Read the Bible. It's for you. Learn more about your Lord and Savior, Jesus Christ. He wants you to know all about Him. Where do you start? You have His Holy Spirit; ask Him.

Simple as that. Welcome to real life. Welcome to the Family.

He who testifies of these things says, "Surely, I come quickly." Amen. Even so, come, Lord Jesus.

The grace of our Lord Jesus Christ be with you all. Amen.

(Revelation 22:20–21)

ABOUT THE AUTHOR

The author was born in Brooklyn, New York.

He is a former middle and high school teacher of science and biology and a real estate broker.

He has a wonderful wife, whom he calls "Kitten," who happens to be his best critic, greatest encourager, and closest friend. They both have seven children together who complete their lives and keep them very busy.

ENDNOTES

1   Romans 8:15

2   Romans 8:17

3   John 14:16

4   Genesis 1:26

5   Psalm 8:5–6

6   Psalm 8:6–9

7   Ezekiel 28:14

8   Isaiah 14:12–19

9   Ezekiel 28:15–19

10   Revelation 6:16–17

11   Proverbs 20:27

12   1 Corinthians 2:11

13   1 Corinthians 2:9–10

14   Genesis 1:28–30, 2:15

15   Genesis 2:16–17

16   Genesis 2:18

17   John 8:44

18   1 Peter 3:7

19   1 Corinthians 11:3

20   1 John 2:16

21   1 Samuel 15:22

22   Genesis 3:7

23	Genesis 3:9, 10
24	Genesis 3:14–24
25	1 Timothy 2:14
26	Romans 3:20
27	1 Corinthians 4:4
28	Romans 8:22
29	Exodus 29:36–37
30	Matthew 26:41
31	James 2:9–11
32	Romans 5:18
33	1 Corinthians 15:45–28
34	Romans 8:32
35	John 1:29, 36
36	Philippians 2:5–7
37	Isaiah 54:7
38	Galatians 3:13
39	2 Corinthians 5:21
40	Luke 23:34
41	2 Corinthians 5:21
42	Isaiah 53:12
43	Hebrews 9:22
44	Romans 8:21–22
45	Acts 20:28
46	Isaiah 53:5
47	Leviticus 17:14

ENDNOTES

48	Deuteronomy 12:23
49	John 8:32, 36
50	Matthew 21:35
51	Zechariah 4:6
52	Acts 10:43
53	2 Timothy 1:7
54	John 15:26
55	Galatians 4:6
56	John 14:26
57	John 16:13–14
58	Romans 5:5
59	Ephesians 4:30–31
60	Ezekiel 36:26–28
61	Psalm 72:14
62	Luke 1:35
63	Romans 3:23
64	Romans 5:12
65	Romans 5:17
66	Romans 5:18
67	Romans 5:19
68	Romans 5:20
69	Romans 5:21
70	John 3:34
71	1 Corinthians 4:4
72	Matthew 2:12

73	Matthew 2:13
74	Psalm 68:19
75	Hosea 11:1
76	Matthew 2:15
77	Matthew 2:19
78	Matthew 2:19–23
79	Ecclesiastes 1:9
80	Deuteronomy 8:3
81	Psalm 91:11–12
82	Deuteronomy 6:16
83	Luke 4:6
84	Deuteronomy 6:13
85	Matthew 15:11, 13
86	Matthew 15:14
87	John 16:27
88	John 15:11
89	Psalm 109:8
90	John 17
91	Matthew 26:36–44
92	Luke 22:43
93	Luke 22:56–60
94	Luke 23:21
95	Luke 22:64
96	Luke 22:67
97	Luke 22:68–69

98   Luke 23:4

99   Luke 23:18

100   Luke 23:34

101   Matthew 27:30

102   Luke 23:22

103   Luke 23:28

104   Luke 23:38

105   Matthew 27:46

106   Luke 23:39

107   Luke 23:41

108   Luke 23:42

109   Luke 23:43

110   Luke 23:46

111   John 19:30

112   1 Corinthians 2:8

113   Acts 1:4–8

114   Matthew 28:18–20

115   Matthew 28–20

116   Acts 1:9-10

117   1 Corinthians 2:8

118   Daniel 11:32

119   Romans 5:8–11

120   Hebrews 11:35

121   Hebrews 11:36

122   Hebrews 11:37